CAPSULE STORIES

Masthead

Natasha Lioe, Founder and Publisher
Carolina VonKampen, Publisher and Editor in Chief
April Bayer, Reader
Hannah Fortna, Reader

Cover art by Darius Serebrova
Book design by Carolina VonKampen

Paperback ISBN: 978-1-953958-02-0
Ebook ISBN: 978-1-953958-03-7

CAPSULE STORIES

Spring 2021 Edition

Contents

Letter from the Editors

And maybe spring will come gently

Maybe it will all come gently

We begin *Capsule Stories Spring 2021 Edition* with these words from Rae Rozman's poem "An Almost Prayer." After such a long, dark winter, with an unrelenting pandemic taking more and more lives every day and political unrest sparking fear and division, spring didn't seem certain this year. It was hard to imagine the world blossoming again; it was hard to remember that such beauty is possible. But it is. Within the pages of this edition, you'll find prose and poetry bursting with life as our contributors explore the theme In Bloom. Spring is here, and with it comes growth, new life, and hope. Maybe it will all come gently.

In Bloom

You are walking down a sidewalk in a park you haven't visited in years. There are too many people, kids running up and down a small grassy hill playing tag with their siblings, adults standing on the pavement. From the top of the hill you look down at the playground, monkey bars with paint barely hanging on. There are too many fingerprints, too many places that were meant to be touched, too many kids sliding down a plastic staticky slide. You take a few steps, and before you realize where you are, you're on the swing set, swinging back and forth through the air, your hands gripped tightly around the metal chains. You throw your head back and let the wind take you. You jump and stick the landing on the rubber floor. Your partner waves at you from the top of the hill. He knows that you're smiling.

As you run back to him, you hold out your hands. Sanitize them. You refuse to touch anything until you can wash your hands at home. But the swing reminds you of something you've been missing. Something you forgot existed, after such a cold winter, a seemingly endless expanse of time with your thoughts. The fog is lifting. The sun is peeking through the clouds. The flowers are starting to bloom.

An Almost Prayer

Rae Rozman

Maybe the leaves
will grow on the trees

And maybe the sunlight
will still warm my garden

And maybe spring will come gently

Maybe it will all come gently

Again, Spring

Darcy Greenwood

You wake
        in a daydream,
slipping from slumber
                into sunshine,
fresh reality blooming
                        everywhere.

Bare branches
        robed in green,
little bluebird singing life
                into something not dead, after all.

Floral corpses revive against a brick wall,
        dewdrops sprinkle young grass with light,
kids play in pretty puddles, watercolor-drenched
                a butterfly flutters with fragile flight.

Everyone sheds layers, breathing again
        air humming with honey hues,
                and all quietly
                        in the gentle wake of spring.

Arriving

Q. Gibson

Rusting beneath the bone of winter
Old silences sleep
A new day is gleaming through
The cracks of dark clouds
The air is light with breath
And the flowers are finding
Their way

Spring's Daughter

Q. Gibson

Boundless in birthing the new
Her cries are a call to the sun's redemption
Full of reclamation
Her seeds have struck beneath the soil
Past seasons are her breeding ground
The rain is her inherited plight
She is the daughter of new beginnings
Her paternal fare is evident in how
She possesses the sun
Her inheritance is everything in bloom
When she is ready
Spring delivers her again

In Loco Parentis

Sue Hann

Someone or something is leaving me messages. Peering out the window in the chilly morning light, waiting for the kettle to boil, I spot white shards of porcelain gleaming like bones against the dark earth in the flowerpot. A trail of soil spills over the rim of the pot and onto the patio, like ellipses. Everything else looks still: the gate is locked; the cherry blossom, long past its flowering season, is stately in dark silhouette. The birds have started their morning song, competing with the oceanic roar of the traffic from the South Circular Road. When the kettle whistles, I take it off the gas before it builds to its strangled scream, and carefully scald the teapot, pondering these cryptic signs.

Tea brewing, I move to the double doors to get a better look. The pieces of porcelain are laid out neatly on the surface of the plant pot, like fossils on display at an archaeological dig. I can make out shards of a saucer that I recognize as my own. I had put them at the bottom of the pot last year to help with drainage before planting tulip bulbs, excited about having a burst of color on the patio come spring. Something colorful to cheer me up when I am looking out the kitchen window doing the washing up. *Maybe baby will be here by then,* I had thought to myself as I planted them.

I did not inherit my father's green fingers. Even that was something he couldn't share. I turned to the internet where I learned about the importance of drainage.

If your pot or planter does not have holes in the base, stones or broken delft can be placed at the bottom to assist with drainage. Carefully, I tipped my pots on their sides to check, and some of them did not have holes. I rooted out some broken bits and pieces of delft from the back of the cupboard—a porcelain spoon that came free with a posh Easter egg, its head now cracked; a saucer with a deep chip; a teacup with a broken handle still nestling in its belly. I took some pleasure in bashing them with the hammer before placing the pieces in the bottom of the planters.

This was my second attempt to plant something outdoors. K and I had neglected our outdoor space since buying the flat, neither of us having much interest in gardening. We inherited a set of planters from the previous owner, square metal things, industrial looking, lined up like sentinels on the kitchen patio. Really patio is too grand a word for the concrete paving slabs, three deep and eight wide, that mark out a chilly north-facing patch of ground outside our flat. It was only during this past year that I took an interest in the garden. I had asked for a Japanese maple sapling as an anniversary gift from K because the leaves always remind me of a shower of crimson stars. We had one in the garden where I grew up. Now that we are trying to conceive, I am nesting perhaps, wanting to nurture life, watch something grow.

At first, we joked, K and I, that it would be funny if I got pregnant immediately, that my Catholic school sex education teacher's warnings about getting pregnant through my tights was right, that K's energetic sperm and my round, bouncy eggs were jumping around at the start line, champing at the bit to get going. We expected this to be the easy part. But one period turned into two and three and four. It frustrated me not knowing what was going on inside the depths of my body. I mean, were we getting close? Is there such thing as nearly pregnant, or way off base, nowhere near pregnant? Were K's sperm almost making it to my egg, and we just needed to be patient? It seemed so mysterious.

How long does it take to get pregnant? I asked Google, as if consulting a medium.

Most couples (eighty-four out of one hundred) will get pregnant within a year if they have regular sex without contraception it replied, via the NHS website. A year! A year seemed like an awfully long time to wait. I was impatient. I researched the lifestyle advice for couples trying to conceive. Caffeine is bad, caffeine does no harm in moderation, coffee is worse than tea for fertility. The differing opinions and facts confused me, so to be safe, I switched to decaf everything. I took my prenatal vitamins, something at least that is not contested, and swallowed them down with hope each day. We both cut down on the little alcohol we drank. I tried harder with my five-a-day fruit and veg. I did my best to turn my body into a hospitable home. Still my body sent me the same message written in blood each month: *no life within.*

When nothing happened after six months, I went in search of more information. In the parenthood section of a large bookstore, I flicked through books promising to "supercharge" or "boost" my fertility or improve my egg quality. I decided that it was time to take things up a notch. I bought an armload of books and started reading one on the bus home.

The dietary advice was bewildering with names of herbs and supplements that I could barely pronounce, agnus castus, amino acid acetyl-L-carnitine, this vitamin at this dose, that mineral at that dose, but not above. I took my list to the health food shop and tried not to look at the total as I typed in my PIN. My kitchen counter was like an apothecary, filled with jars and bottles and pills in blister packs. I swallowed them all down.

I read my fertility books in bed, pencil in hand, underlining, as if in preparation for an exam: *egg quality, fertility charts, cervical fluid.* I started tracking my basal body temperature, cervical fluid, and bleeds using an app on my phone. I felt like my own science experiment.

"Why do I have to do all of this?" I grumbled, as K sat beside me in bed reading his comic on the iPad.

The fact that I haven't managed to keep anything alive in the garden or in my body is dispiriting. Earlier in the year, I bought a packet of seeds, cosmos, because I liked their name and the internet said that they were easy to grow. *They can be planted directly outside once any risk of frost has passed*, it said. I scattered the seeds in the dark earth, covered them with soil, and watered them in, confidently expecting a riot of color by early summer. The packet said that they should be flowering within fifty to sixty days. Eating dinner in the garden on the long summer evenings, I inspected the soil for any sign of green shoots. Nothing. Maybe it was the soil? Did I overwater them? Was it the weather? Coming from Central and South America, they like hot weather; maybe the summer wasn't hot enough for them? Their failure to grow remained a mystery to me.

My father had green fingers. Always growing houseplants from cuttings—spider plants, Busy Lizzies—or going to the garden center to buy bedding plants for outside. He did a lot better with plants than he did with people. Without much effort, things grew for him. I could do with some of his advice now. I fantasize about how we might go to the garden center down the road. He would know what to get, what to plant where. I daydream, knowing it is just that; a dream where he is a different father, a different person with a different past. Trying for a baby has made me think more about my own parents in a way I had not expected.

When I don't conceive after more than a year, I make an appointment at my GP office. Surely now it is time for some answers? I have waited and waited with a prepped and primed body, loaded with vitamins, healthy food, and every supplement going. The office is chilly, and the other patients keep their coats buttoned up in the waiting area. Everyone eyes the display screen that beeps every few minutes and announces the name of the next patient.

Finally, it's my turn. It's a GP I haven't seen before. They seem to come and go from this busy practice. As she looks up from her screen, I guess that we're about the same age.

"We've been trying to conceive for over a year now with no success," I tell her. She asks me about my periods, and I reach for my phone to pull up the information on my fertility app.

"Get rid of the app," she says. "You need to be having sex every two to three days, and forget the app."

I try to explain that I have done my research on this, that I am following all the advice and using the app to record my information. I'm not blindly following the directions of this app like an electronic deity and only having sex on my so-called fertile days, which is, I assume, the conclusion she has come to in these past few seconds.

"Get rid of it," she repeats, dismissively. "You're still young. In the thirty-five to thirty-nine age bracket, 90 percent of couples conceive naturally after two years, so just keep going." Now there is another goalpost: two years.

She types something into her screen, and as she half stands to adjust the cable at the back of her monitor, I can see her swelling belly. She is heavily pregnant. Her bump sits between us, tauntingly. I wonder how easy it was for her to get pregnant.

"I wouldn't worry too much. Keep trying and come back to us if things don't improve."

It is a few days later that I spot the leaver of messages. It is facedown in the planter, squatting on its hind legs, wind milling its forelimbs into the soil, digging, digging, digging. The shards of porcelain are pushed to one side of the pot and a squirrelly tail hangs over the side, luxuriantly fluffy. This close, I can see how fine the hairs of the tail are, almost diaphanous. Its body is surprisingly muscular. I'm not sure if the squirrel is in the process of trying to find my bulbs to eat or whether he is busy hiding his own food in my pot. Either way, he is a threat to my flowers. I bang hard on the glass and the squirrel freezes, stock-still, assessing the danger. Then, in that funny jerky, stop-motion way that squirrels have, it looks right and left, and deciding there is no threat, continues plowing into the soil, scattering dirt all over the patio.

I turn to the internet again for advice on protecting bulbs from squirrels. They don't like daffodil bulbs, one website tells me. Is this what gardening is? Does everyone else go to all of this trouble just for a few flowers? I didn't think it was going to be this much of a faff. *Fine, one more try. Daffodils it is.*

In the garden center with K, I select a few nets of daffodil bulbs from the rack then stand in front of the bags of compost, studying them, trying to remember what I have read about the environmental dangers of compost with peat in it. There are different brands and different types: multipurpose, moisture control, enriched. I have no idea which one I need. I choose one at random. The bag is awkwardly heavy as K lugs it the short distance back to our flat.

I cut open the plastic sack of compost, and the smell is rich with the promise of life. It feels nicely cool and moist in my hands as I fill the planters with the dark loam. Making pockets in the earth with my trowel, I lower the bulbs gently as babies, cradling them to make sure they are root side down in their cozy nests before covering them with a fresh blanket of compost.

My mother loves to tell a story about me gardening as a child. I am six years old, playing in the garden with my toy set of garden tools, a small trowel, a tiny garden fork. I am happily stabbing them in the earth, squatting down, watching muck go everywhere. My mother is kneeling beside me, about to sow some seeds. Then with her adult-sized trowel, she makes shallow holes in the earth. Seeing a teachable moment, she leans over to show me the packet of seeds.

"See, this is how a baby is made. A seed grows into a baby."

I look at her skeptically. "Last time you said it was an egg."

I go back to my digging, giving up on this very unreliable narrator. My mother loves to tell this story, as evidence of one precocious child and one mother who mixed her metaphors once too often. K loves this story. "You are always disagreeable, even as a child!" He is delighted with himself. I smile to myself, remembering his reaction, and my hand goes to my belly, hoping that this seed and this egg have stuck this time.

Throughout the winter, I wonder what's going on in the planters, wonder what my little bulbs are doing. In my mind I can see their egg-yolk yellow cheeriness next spring. For now, I wait for signs of life. *This is the last chance*, I tell them. *You are squirrel resistant, bedded into a nice nutrient-rich home. Sprout life,* I urge them silently, one hand cupping my flat belly. *Sprout life.* Then I wait for the first signs.

this spring

Lotte van der Krol

this spring I'll only sow wildflowers
nothing edible
nothing useful
nothing productive
nothing that needs my attention or my effort
nothing that needs tending or staking or potting or
     weeding or cutting or trimming
nothing that needs me
just
wild
wild
wildflowers
and when the grass is high and rustling
I'll let flowers grow through my hair
through my fingers
my open palms
let myself be buried in fallen petals
burrow down in the dying grass
and eventually
let new grasses grow
all over
me

Watching Grass Grow

Madi Giovina

It sounds
boring
but it is
necessary.
To see
life made
out of
nothing.
Death has
higher
cinematic
value.
A slow
choke. A
deep cut.
Our hands
are capable
of so much
pain.
Grass, it
just grows.
In one
direction:
toward the sun.
And instead
of watching,
we trample
it. These
are not
the blades
that excite us.

Stewart Mineral Springs

Madi Giovina

I wonder if trees
envy youth as humans do.
Hate their girth as it

reveals their age. Or
if the young trees aspire
to grow tall someday,

too, to see more rain
-storms and shooting stars, to reach
closer to the sky

Off-Green Thumb

Madi Giovina

I   tend   to   hurt

                              my   own   feelings.

I don't intend   to,   but
    I   tend   to.

                    I   am   soft   &
                                    I   prick   myself
          with   sharp,   needle-like   thoughts
and   stinging   self-talk.

I need to tend   to   myself.
To   my   soft, tender   self.
          Like   I   tend   to   my
                                        philodendron:
          with water and just enough sunlight,
          with water and just enough sunlight.

          Tend   to   myself.
To   my   soft, tender   self.

I   intend   to;

I Told You It Takes Me Hours to Water My House-plants

AJ Buckle

Because every time I do could be the last
so I sing to each one
individually.
Every one gets a name,
a special hello
and goodbye
just in case.
You said
"That's stupid,
they're just plants."
And that made me
feel small.

Because I always forget
the finality of things.
And when one dies,
it's my fault.
It's a constant reminder
to be attentive
even in the smallest places.

In Buddhist tradition
there is the concept of mujō where
one must think of impermanence
constantly.
And when I water my plants
I do.
Because each one deserves
an individual bit of grace.

Strange how even the
inconsequential things
become important when you're alone.
So I take hours to water my plants
because for now,
they're here.
And you're not.

a constant reminder
to be attentive

even in the
smallest places

Phoebe Bridgers

AJ Buckle

On our first date
I showed up enraptured,
a momentous disaster.
My nerves had gotten the better of me
as they always do.
I asked what record you had playing
and you told me
the album was called *Punisher*,
which seemed fitting.
It needed to be flipped, but
I had trouble focusing
on anything save for
eyes like spring twilight.
When you leaned in,
I was dying to taste your lips.
And then the dog was locked away,
our mutual demons
were being kept at bay, and
you climbed on to me.
I ran my hands up your thighs
to the small of your back and
felt the shiver of
fluorescents flickering on,
of moths opening wings
after having freshly emerged
from cocoons.
I caught flame and trembled,
because your skin was so new.

And to me,
it was like delicately running my fingers
over a newly healed wound.
Like young blossoms
shivering at the first taste
of the spring rain.
Everything was delicate.
I watched the leaves
outside your window
and was humbled.
And I
I keep thinking about
your hands
on my body.

I keep thinking about

your hands

on my body

Crown Shyness

AJ Buckle

As a phenomenon in trees,
the reasons for crown shyness aren't known,
but the speculation is that
interdigitation between canopy branches
leads to reciprocal pruning
between related and unrelated species.

I focus on the hesitancy of touch
rather than the touch itself.
It is a constant dance of attrition,
where I never know the correct steps.
It's an adaptive behavior
I'm trying to break.

In windy areas,
trees suffer physical damage
as they collide
with one another.
As a result of the abrasions,
crown shyness is a response.

And strangely,
this feeling is ineffable,
though I've been there before.

Think of first dates,
think of holding hands with a new lover.
No, actually,
think of desperately wanting to do so,
but being unable to for fear of
unwittingly damaging them.

On warm days
I lie naked in the forest
and look up to the tops of trees.
I weave my fingers through the grass
for practice at
trying to be gentle.

The canopy resembles islands
I could get lost in,
with rivers of sky cutting through.
And I watch the branches lazily dancing
in the breeze and wish
to be carried away with the leaves.
And I silently curse everything
that keeps me anchored here.
But the trees survive,
they survive
and so must I.

I weave my fingers through the grass
for practice at trying to be gentle

Family Tree

K-Ming Chang

Everyone in Shereen's family was born first as a tree.
It began centuries ago, when women first began eating soil to bury the hunger in their bellies. The soil was seasoned with salt and rain and belonged to a salt merchant who was known for his many wives, eight hundred of them, all of whom ranged from ages zero to ninety-five. The babies were raised and presented to him at the age of fifteen, and the eldest of them were employed as his caretakers. All his wives spent every night salting their chests to preserve their olived nipples. One of his wives, the first of Shereen Hui's ancestors, was three years old when she was sold to the household. A decade later, the salt merchant summoned her aboard his leisure boat, a hollow tree shaped like a flicking finger, and when she refused, he ordered her to be tied to a tree and forced to swallow hot oil. While tied to the tree, she remembered the only thing that was spoken to her by her first family, the one she was shuttled away from, a story about women who survived a famine by consuming a type of black soil—pebbled with bones and scrubbed by the sun—that erased all aches when you swallowed a handful of it. The roots of the tree she was roped to—its vines were thick and velvet as antlers—reached down into the dirt at her feet and spooned the soil into her mouth. After feeding her a fistful, the tree's limbs pried open the knot around her wrists, and Shereen's foremother was freed. She spent the rest of her lifetime fleeing from city to city, reminding the locals that eating certain soils would ensure survival.

Sometime in the Song dynasty, according to the rain's research, there were books about citizens who opened their legs and gave birth to beech trees, bodhi trees, eucalyptus saplings too, as well as the occasional ash (though this is just a footnote that the rain types on all our roofs). The trees fingered out the ground root-first, then their trunks, then their branches with

elbows for bending and scratching and slapping away mosqui-
toes. When the tree was replanted—preferably in soil that was at
least as wet as a human mouth—the trees cleaved open on their
own, fully-grown children inside. There were some who stayed
inside their trees for years, like Shereen, whose trunk slivered
open when she was fourteen. The tree didn't know how to walk,
only how to kneel, how to imitate birds with its branches, how
to make sound by scratching away the scabs of its bark.

Shereen's family rented a house in Montebello with a yard
wide enough to sprout several siblings side by side; Shereen's
sisters split out of their trunks by the age of seven, a fact that
Shereen's mother, Birchy, repeated daily. *When you were a tree,
you grew so slow, we had to wait for you to reach my waist,* she told
Shereen. She complained about Shereen's prenatal tendency to
secrete sap, how her tree always had to squat over a bucket or
staunch a kitchen towel between her root-legs. Even after Sher-
een emerged from her tree, sap hardened to coins along her
calves and the inside of her thighs, selling its sweetness to flies.

Shereen, fourteen and newly hatched from her tree,
watched her mother burn the bark in the backyard. It was a
family ritual to gather the remnants of the trunk and branches
to roast them ripe, ax them to ash. Shereen rallied the smoke
into her fists, shaped it into a sundress, and wore that until
her mother said, *Don't you dare walk naked out of this house or
I will bark you back into a tree.* Shereen was not offended by
this threat, and in fact preferred her treehood, the years when
her roots were metallic in sunlight, the birds polka-dotting
her skin with their droppings, the occasional neighborhood
children who snuck into the yard to climb her, falling when
she shrugged. Children who spat their teeth like dice, who
chanced gravity, who cooed at crows as if everything under-
stood them, who etched their family names into her trunk

with their fingernails, names she looked for later on her skin but could not find, and so at night she traced alphabet shapes onto her bare belly, touched herself aloud.

Shereen's mother told her never to show anyone her belly. She and her sisters were missing something called a button. *A button like this*, Shereen's mother said, lifting her shirt and drawing a circle the size of a wedding ring in the center of herself. Shereen reached forward and smeared it with her thumb, collapsed the circle into a cloud.

Birchy deemed herself a tree-woman of purpose. Even as a young tree, she frequently littered her limbs, donating herself to firewood, despite the fact that no one in Southern California required firewood. During the wildfires every summer, Shereen's mother raised her roots into stilts and forked up portions of the fire with her boughs, walking the fire out of the city, despite the fact that later the city would deem walking trees illegal, fining Birchy eight hundred dollars. Shereen learned years later than her mother never outgrew this fine, that when she failed to pay it, she was jailed for three months until her two sisters stole enough car radios to pay her bail.

When you park your car, Shereen's mother specified, *duct tape your windows so no one can see what's in it*. When Shereen told her mother that this didn't seem to deter thievery, her mother scrubbed at her cheek with a thumb and said, *You're a smart girl, but you have to listen to someone who's been stolen from.*

Shereen turned fifteen and graduated into speech, but it was the kind of speech that others mistook for minced meat. Shereen was schooled in silences: there was the silence of the trunk she was born swathed inside, the silence after a siren, the silence of wildfire smoke, all the rich women evacuating their mansions while Shereen's mother ran through the house, filling a bathtub with soy milk, telling her and her sisters to duck inside of it, to hold their breaths inside that white. She plugged the door cracks with wet T-shirts, beat back the smoke with the broom, while up in the hills the mansions married themselves to the sky, smoke fluttering like blonde hair against their windows.

Always remember, Birchy said, *how flammable you are.* It was months after her birth from tree-form when Birchy finally told her: *The one thing we keep from all our years of being trees. Is that we burn. We burn as fast as this,* Shereen's mother said, beating an egg yolk to snot. Nipping a fly into her fist. Plucking out her own white hairs and burning them in the bathtub. All fire-producing fuels, including soybean oil, were stored in tubs behind the chili bushes in the backyard, and matches were strictly prohibited. Birthday candles were canceled as a concept. *Imagine,* Shereen's mother said, curling her hair in front of the bathroom mirror. The hair curlers and their heater were the only permissible electronics; all others, including televisions and space heaters and anything else with stray wiring, were deemed a danger. Birchy's cosmetology bag, which she toted to clients' houses, was illicit with wiring: the straightener, the curlers, the eyelash electrifier that promised sparks when you blinked at your man. *Imagine if you blew out those candles and corralled it into your sisters' hair and we all caught fire. Always keep your breath to yourself,* Shereen's mother said.

The summer Shereen was fifteen, her mother took her and her two older sisters to a redwood forest. They drove through Scotts Valley, past townhouses painted bright as cloves of garlic, the kind of house where girls rusted on swing sets and mothers wore aprons and the trees were not only wicks, instead crocheting the fog around the houses. Roadside, the redwood trees were so wide that the light could not reach around their waists, so tall that Shereen looked up and saw only the fog. Shereen's sisters knocked on the trunks, listening for the responding knocks of children inside, but their mother said that these trees were too old to hatch children. *They were here before the houses*, their mother said, stepping over a root thicker than her thigh. *And we were trees before there were women.*

One of Shereen's sisters was a birch like their mother, and another was a sycamore, skinny-limbed and light-skinned, trunks smooth as a waxed shin. Because Shereen had been burred and furred, her sisters called her Furry, though Shereen was not offended: the trees she loved best were the ones with knotted spines, too many limbs and joints, bark thick and scaled, the kind that burns slow. Beyond nicknames, neither of her sisters spoke to her; they were wary of Shereen, the only one who didn't split from treehood until she was already a teen. *A girl like that*, First Birch Sister said, *is unnatural.* First Birch Sister and Sycamore drew belly buttons on their bare stomachs with liquid eyeliner and sometimes a laundry marker, but when their mother saw them comparing buttons in the mirror, each of them drawing theirs larger and larger until their bellies were shaded entirely, she laughed and told her daughters: *You drew them blue.* When the sisters asked what color belly buttons were, and whether it was possible to construct them out of chicken skin, their mother said, *It's not a color. It's a hole in you.* That night, First Birch Sister and Sycamore swiped knives from the kitchen and stood in front of the mirror, daring each other to go first, go first, core it out, a little hole, but neither of them could decide on the size nor the depth, whether it should be the size of a button on the back of a dress or the button of an elevator. In the end, the sisters fell asleep on either side of Shereen, their knives neighboring her spine.

The summer of the redwood trees, of limbs long enough to floss out the moon, another family moved into the duplex next door, a mother and father and daughter, a family of no trees, all of them born with buttoned bellies. The daughter's name was Yasuko, and because her yard was bare as a kneecap, not even a potted kumquat tree, and because she also had no TV, and because it was summer and she knew no one from the high school Shereen would soon attend, Yasuko did nothing but squat on the driveway and spit into the cracks, watching her saliva river down to the street, a crooked seam.

Shereen remembered the silence inside a trunk, the way it was to be wood, wooed by winds, reining in the rain, sewing into the dirt what the rest of the world was illiterate in: thirst. Shereen got a job that summer doing yardwork, something that did not require words, and though she knew the neighbor grew nothing, she wanted a way to approach Yasuko. She knocked on the door and regretted her knuckles. In her hands was a pair of pruning shears, and she wondered who had pruned her as a tree, if it was her mother who parted her leaves and plucked out the dying ones, who checked her branches for rot.

When Yasuko answered, Shereen shut the shears in her right hand. They snipped together, a silver sound, and Shereen winced to hear it. Her first word to Yasuko: scissoring. But Yasuko smiled, asking if she could hold the shears, if she could try them out, and Shereen placed them in her palms. Yasuko lifted the shears to her own hair, a ponytail that batted from side to side, and Shereen gasped to see the strands severed. But Yasuko laughed, returning the shears, and stepped over the stain of her own hair in the doorway. *Let's go somewhere,* Yasuko said, and Shereen wanted to say that going places was antithetical to her body, that having been born a tree, she was an expert in remaining still, a whole lifetime lassoed into one spot, rings stacking inside her like unwashed dishes.

They sat together on the driveway. Yasuko's face was all friction, her palms pebbled with callouses even though she rarely worked, except to sometimes waitress at her parents' restaurant downtown. Shereen explained that she dined mostly on dirt, that this had begun dynasties ago, and Yasuko laughed, laying the shears down on the driveway as gently as a bird she had rehabilitated. The shadow of the blades on the pavement feathered like wings. *I got these callouses because I grip my hairbrush so hard*, Yasuko said, *and my mother always tells me to let go, loosen up. I'm glad you gave me a way to cut my hair.* Shereen stroked the shears, lifting them into her lap, and made a fist so that she wouldn't reach up and touch Yasuko's newly bare neck, the blue birthmark on the side of it.

Yasuko stood up and toed at the sidewalk, her shadow all shoulders, and asked Shereen how long she'd been eating dirt. *Is it a Chinese thing?* she asked. She said she once watched a documentary about something like this, a festival of people eating pottery. Yasuko said she wanted to try. *Do you think people ever eat scissors? What's a place where people do that?* she asked. Shereen felt her shadow curdle beneath her. *China*, Shereen said, knowing it wasn't true. That was what Shereen's mother told her: when someone asks you a question, respond with a country. *Say you're American*, she said, *and no one can touch you.* Though Shereen knew this wasn't true: once, outside the Ranch 99 in Monterey Park, a man with two moles above his forehead stood beside the rows of toy vending machines, the kind that spat Pokémon keychains and Sailor Moon erasers out of their mouths. While her mother was inside lifting each egg to the light—you have to check and see if there are chicks inside them, she said—Shereen watched the machines. Feed it a quarter and crank the yellow handle, a toy bulbed inside a plastic sphere.

The man with two moles said to Shereen, *If you come here and hold my hand, I'll buy you one of these.* He pointed at the Sailor Moon machine, each of the toy-eggs jostling inside, and rummaged both his pockets with his fists. When Shereen offered her hand for him to hold, he gripped her wrist and kneaded his crotch against her palm. Shereen jerked away, turning away, but he said, *Just wait, just wait.* It was Shereen's mother who chased the man away, revving her shopping cart and running at him like a raccoon Shereen had seen once, chasing a mutt down the street, head low and teeth penciled. It was Shereen's mother who asked: *Why didn't you scream?* Her mother tugged at her wrist harder than any man, treating her arm like a leash. She gave Shereen a plastic whistle and told her to blow it whenever she was alone. That night, between her sisters, she gripped the whistle between her teeth and blew until her mother manifested in the doorway and agreed to sleep beside her, her mother who was no longer a tree but still had the shade of one, casting herself across the house.

Yasuko, upon hearing this story, told Shereen to always carry her shears. *But what about you?* Shereen asked. *What will you carry? My hands,* Yasuko said, *my hands are enough.* They were planetary hands, Yasuko explained, larger than her older brother's, her brother who left for sea. *A sailor?* Shereen asked, but Yasuko said no, he was a swimmer whose goal was to swim inside each of the world's seven seas. So far, he had swum in all of them except for the Arctic Ocean and the Indian Ocean, and he was in the Arctic now, where it was night during the day, when afternoons were the color of steeped tea. *Won't he be cold,* Shereen asked, but Yasuko said he carved open a seal and swam inside its carcass, emptying its organs and slipping his limbs inside the fat-pouched flippers. He would be buoyed by another body. Shereen thought she understood: being with

Yasuko felt like that, like making room in her body for another one. Like she was a baby pearled inside a tree, crouched inside another life, doubled.

Yasuko taught Shereen how to make a rope swing, except instead of rope they used Yasuko's severed hair, braiding it thick as a wrist and knotting it to the limb of a birch. *The trick is to let go*, Yasuko said, *when you're the highest you can go*. Shereen gripped the length of Yasuko's hair and ran to propel herself, swinging back and forth, and when she was above the street, Shereen let go. She landed on the blacktop, her shoulder-bone crumpling beneath her, but even after she blacked out and Yasuko had to drag her home, even after she woke up in her sisters' bed with a towel laid over her face like she was dead, with her mother leaning over and saying, *If you die, don't come back as a ghost and blame me*, Shereen believed the tree had reached for her. Believed the branches swung toward her like a dozen braids of white hair, begging for her to grip them and hold on. But Shereen refused to reach for them, instead choosing to suspend, choosing the street and Yasuko, breakage over faith. The birch remembered her and said, *Don't you remember when you were inside us, how free you were from feeling*. Below on the street, Yasuko laughed and waved both hands. Shereen chose to land.

When she was home in bed for three days, her shoulder swaddled in two bags of frozen fish filets from landing on it, Yasuko visited and sat by her beside. Shereen told her the story of the woman in the Song dynasty, the first of their lineage to birth trees, then said, *Aren't you the one who's supposed to be telling me stories?* Yasuko laughed and agreed, then resumed the story of her brother who swam in the Pacific and stole it like a skirt, flipping up its hem. He saw its coral reefs like bruised fingertips, its fish the size of women. *He swam the whole thing?* Shereen asked, and Yasuko nodded. Lungs the size of lecture halls. His feet broad as those fish that swim on their sides in the dark, the kind you could buy at Dahua and fry with lime. When Shereen dreamed those three days, it was of the trees plucking her up, hanging her like rain.

After her shoulder could swing again, Shereen's mother called her to help in the kitchen, handing her a knife to butterfly the fish. *A sad family*, she said to Shereen, nodding next door. *They used to have a son.* Her mother was cutting stiff tofu in the palm of her hand, layering it with her blade. She placed the knife down and walked to Shereen, the tofu glowing in her palm like a stroked animal, and said, *If you're ever sad, remember your auntie from the Song dynasty. Eat dirt and become another living thing. A tree. Anything.*

That afternoon, when she knocked on Yasuko's door, Shereen did not mention the dead brother or his collection of oceans. She remembered the last story Yasuko told at her bedside: about a boy named Momotaro who was born from a peach. His village was terrorized by a giant who lived on a purple-dirt hill and kidnapped children to feast on their belly buttons. But Momotaro, because he was born from a peach and possessed no belly button, was the only boy in the village exempt from danger. He donned a sword and a spear and climbed the hill of purple dirt and beheaded the giant and returned the children still living. Shaggy with sleep, Shereen had said she was the same, that she had no belly button, and as she shut her eyes, she felt Yasuko lift the hem of her shirt.

When Yasuko answered the door, she reached out both hands and flicked up the hem of Shereen's shirt, confirming that her belly was tofu-blank. *Do you still have the shears?* Yasuko asked, and Shereen nodded. *We could slit you one, a belly button*, Yasuko said, but Shereen said that in the story, her blank belly had saved her from the giant. *You're not Momotaro*, Yasuko said. Momotaro was a boy and a peach and his teeth

---

were neat. *If this were a story,* Shereen said, *you would get eaten and I would be spared.*

But Yasuko said this was not a story. She pointed at the birch tree, her rope-braid of hair still dangling from the lowest branch, and Shereen told her to cut it down or a woman would grow from it. *From what,* Yasuko said, but Shereen remembered her lives as a tree. In the Song dynasty, there was a woman tied to the trunk of Shereen. Lives later, there was a girl hanged from her branches, left there by the Japanese, naked. In all her lives as a tree, her limbs were complicit in gravity.

Sighing, Yasuko said she would cut down her hair from the tree and resew it to her scalp. *If that's what you want,* she said, and Shereen was relieved. They sat together on the chapped driveway. Shereen turned to Yasuko and asked how her brother learned water. Yasuko talked about the beach, about her brother sunburned with skin shucked off him like bark, of the heat fevers, how the sea looked impossible to be split into seven, but that was before she knew severance.

Shereen listened. The day she'd decided to surrender her treehood, there was lightning. It was summer. Lightning strung across the sky and turned trees into smoke-ribbons, into cored apples, into braids of bleached hair. Before then, Shereen hadn't wanted to see the sky, but it spoke to her that day, stroked her trunk with fingers of light. *You're right about how cold it must be in the Arctic Ocean,* Yasuko said, *and lonely.* Without answering, Shereen reached for Yasuko's fists, unfurling them in her lap, remembering these fingers, the lightning when it entered her, the trunk opening like a corset to birth her. She looked up at the sky and wondered if it was really the reflection of the sea. How this couldn't be true when they were so far from any water big enough to wade into. Across from her, Yasuko reached up, resting her knuckles against Shereen's cheek, summing up the sky in that touch.

The Sun Will Rise

Purnima Bala

The sun will rise another day, my love,
even beyond our shuttered eyes, these
blossoms growing into timeless peace,
the world passing us by. Listen—that bird
calls out not knowing if another hears it.

(Does it ask for help?)   I'm here,

I know you. We see the same sky screaming
in colors: for belief and for prayers. Passion
that protests on the streets. For dreams gone
cold. I know what it's like when your body
no longer feels at home and your mind is a
black hole.

(Does the bird seem lonely to you?)

Let your fingers linger in mine a little longer.
I plead—stay. Stay with the scent of orange
peel, with drifting dandelion seeds, with the
whisper of trees spilling secrets to the wind.

You don't need to speak—I'll wait.
And when the stars come alive, I'll pour
salt into my mouth, bury my tongue beneath
memories   so it won't lose itself.

But the sun will rise another day, my love.
I hope you will too. Just once more, once more,
once, once again.

Crickets in the Bathroom

Eli Vandell

We're meant to kill you, little Virginia
cricket burrowing in carpets
as you burrow in fields.

You tap your legs together
in soft clamor, composing
a ditty for the basement walls.

Yet we let you sing, let you croon
blurry-eyed as we stumble inside
the bathroom, barely noticing

how you lie watching
from the corner, antennae
still as stone. i ask

my darling, *do you love
me?* and his *i do* echoes
and roots in my mouth,

becomes a litany, hair still
smelling of smoke, his tongue
like wheat—an encore,

like the cricket's legs
your delicate song,
i do, i do, i do

Appalachian Symphony

Eli Vandell

---

i.

your God's favorite time

is the moment   is the morning

between blue and green   you can tell the difference

ii.

as you walk you think

a beaten body   is a good body

is anything but   a good body

not   beaten

iii.

your skin is a pool

of cicada spit and ash   water under roots

still bubbling   and suds in the dirt

an orifice   of Earth

iv.

press your tongue

to Pan's flute tip   to fairy circle stones

and wait for   and let

your throat   glow

Lover as Leviathan

Eli Vandell

---

i. will you gorge yourself on the body that was once heedful of your admiration?

my lover's mouth sets alight some foolish tremor
on this grief-soaked skin of mine.
like gods, we tumble across the Earth, gulping rivers
in our rush to consume the other,
not knowing who will be killed before the next sunrise.

your gaze pretends to comprehend this monstrous body,
for hidden inside these glutinous roots
seeps a soliloquy, unheard
for seven days and forty nights, three times over
before the birth of your own destruction.

even in roughness, as we roll in grit,
you cup my face like a goblet,
its holy contents too precious
to drink.

ii. will you swallow my pickled skin when the world ends?

there is nothing more tender
than a jawline;
unhinged, it envelops,
softly molding the contours
of your unspilled breath.

---

the hazardous design
of this life, how we succeed on slipping
across the line dividing satiety
and surfeit,
making our beds over the borders of halcyon
and deluge.

iii. do you hold on your tongue only that which you adore?

come, beloved, open the glass,
tip back your throat;
the only way
we are allowed

to love is
to devour.

to love is
to devour

three bodies

BEE LB

chase each other through the world,
green swallowing their legs as they
bound across open space, a spiraling
dance through wind. three bodies

draw near, splay out in a welcomed
frenzy. neck craning to follow, to
trace movement through time,
stopping short of the past. a fragment

caught by sight, bodies collapsing in
a pile of strain, blue air stretching
endless above them. freedom found
in hands caressing a warm life

pulling to match the tense expectation
the bodies lift in reverse, stumble up,
straining against the act
of being halved by earth.

springtide

BEE LB

a voice carrying in the wind, deep and
genuine and free, paramount

hand gripping arm as i fall
unaware

of the significance of touch

your skin meeting my own

the distance that comes with
a glimpse of you, heart stutters

laughter bursting, breath catches,
always, always, imagine now

a wish, a misunderstanding,
the cage we've left our voices in,

the knowing look, the shared secrets,
our voices ours alone, meant for the two

of us together, moving, gliding, growing

and then not. the wish, again,
left unanswered, your hand on mine

the memory, the present lack of you
your voice, your overwhelming

presence, left here,
an enclave, still
waiting to be
found

the cherished body

BEE LB

after Nikki Giovanni

life does not swell beneath my fingers
when it is my fingers touching your heart
or your chest, the cage that contains your heart

warmth settles over me and it is not easy;
my breath stutters under the weight of what i feel
for you, the need resting heavy in my chest. i'll tangle
my life with yours and call it love. when i can't hold the
eye of my attachment i'll call that desire. touch my lips
to the connection between us and call it devotion
does this sound like a need too big to fill

when your arms are empty of my waiting body,
your body seeks mine out, your touch made ecstatic
with the hunger of my body finding yours. my lips beg for
the closeness that only you can provide, the words catch beneath
my tongue and you coax them out as formless sound,
your lips softening against my need. if i'm indebted
to my desires, your desires are mine as well

trill

BEE LB

---

an offering of peace, laced into each our careful words
the branch stretched between our two mouths

this small hope clung to our hands, keeping us holding
still to each other, inaction to the point of sanctimony

we touch our bodies and imagine in them the other, this
hold so tender it may soon disappear into blushing bruise

i see in you something so unfathomable, the secret
of what could last, nestled between your fragile eyes

admittance

BEE LB

the long trail down, heart racing against rails as you rush
through the hills to find
something better—
                    clean air,
                            cheap fuel,
                                    bitter coffee—
                                            every hint leading back
brushed under heavy cover. the faint tremble
of a lifeline, grasping
                    for any familiar touchstone
                            lacking perfection but
                                    offering necessary comfort—

not yet knowing which endings were meant to be final, or the
consequences of opening closed doors
nevermind that, there is
                    salt in the air
                            a memory of blue lips
                                    in a freezing ocean
                                            unfurls over your tongue
and you can't help the rush of fondness seeping into your
chest as you weep at the peak
                    oh this delicate start,
                            this fragile hold,
                                    this dizzying confusion
                                            at the possibility of being
                                                    free

Camano Island Sunrise

Emily Iris Degn

Linen sheets basked in dawn,
flittering in the cold air of the morning.
The meadow grass sits in lush tufts
at the foot of the laundry basket,
soaked in dew and last night's thoughts.
The brisk blue sky licks the heavens
in a quenching cerulean,
like a crown for early risers.

The Dawn of Spring

Katherine Wiles

Clouds drift and silken
moonlight rests briefly in the spring darkness.
Miniscule hairs sparkle like stars
and the scent of growing grass
envelops me.

The blazing dawn beautifies all,
the ecstasy of its glory lingering
throughout the day.
I watch barefoot from the dewy lawn,
newly green, and soak in
the growing colors
and the new warmth
of the sun.

The Gatherers

Katherine Wiles

April blossoms stand tall, monuments
to rain and sun.
Silver voices ring
in the garden, echo across the sky.
Children dart like sparrows through the grass,
swoop like hawks on the flowers,
gather them in bunches for bouquets,
cultivars and weeds blended indiscriminately.

Persephone Practices Social Distancing in the Underworld

Natalia A. Pagán Serrano

you're surprised when you see them:
last time, they sprung
while you were watching
and now, you've missed it—
the blooming

you can't be angry, of course
the seasons don't ask for permission
to pass. you've cheated yourself
out of it, the world's rebirth

maybe you should have left
with more frequency, but no

while it all takes on color, you unfurl
before the sun. this time, not even the call
to harvest can lure you out.

today your
twenty-
year-old
self reminds
you home is
beautiful

Natalia A. Pagán Serrano

---

flowers fall on the island too
pink dust crowding parking spaces

you've erased this fact or refused
to remember it—

do you hear it? the wind has forgotten
your name.

I Think It's Spring, Can You Look It Up?

Natalia A. Pagán Serrano

home never taught me the signs:
the birds returned all at once,
like they'd caught the same flight back
from wherever they'd been.

the sky's attempting to be more blue
than the blue of the place you birthed
me into, and no other.

sidewalks flush and I take pictures
for you. you say,
narcisos, silvestres, lilas.
I say, *yellow daffodils, bubblegum peonies,*
lavender lilacs, desert mariposa lilies.

I wonder how they will take
this leftover cold. Mami,
did you find anything?

the birds are at my window,
sounding some joy that belongs
in places bluer than this.

you say, *Mándame fotos*
I say, *I already sent them*
you say, *Wow*
I'm glad we're seeing this together.

In Florence

Emma Bider

The shrubs in the Giardino Torrigiani are meticulously shaped, the center lawn a paradise of manicured green and marble figures dotting the pathways with what I assume is artistic precision. There is little shade. I worry about Adela, who did not bring an umbrella. The statues of people I've never heard of, but my mother-in-law has, bore me a little. We came to see the flowers.

Our tour guide sits us down in a corner of the botanical garden with angular rows of herbs and other medicinal plants. He directs our eyes first to the hibiscus flowers, their drowsy yellow and red petals used to make tea, then to a clutch of blue lavender and invites us to gently brush it with our hands and breathe in the exquisite aroma. We enter a greenhouse bursting with pinks, purples, oranges, and reds. The roof is stained glass, the heat surprising for its depth, as though the air is thrumming with the breath of a hundred living things.

The back wall of the greenhouse is covered in tillandsia—air plants, says Adela—their long, delicate fronds ending in vivid reds. A few of the bigger ones, resting in the branches of a small tree, have sprouted flowers that resemble birds of paradise. Adela eyes them with a big smile. We both gravitate toward the smallest specimens, almost hidden behind the others. She mutters something to the effect of *what is there to fear when such beauty exists?* and I reply without thinking, "Being unremarkable."

At first, I think I must have gotten the Italian wrong because she says nothing, and then my mind goes to Luciano, taking pictures of only the most beautiful things. Adela looks for a long time at the smallest tillandsia resting on a narrow shelf. It is green and speckled white. It could fit in my hand. I join her and ask her to tell me all about it, and she does, gladly.

Present Tense

Kersten Christianson

This morning's first thought,
how sweet the wind, summer
bloom of iris, rugosa, blue
harebells, beach peas.

Tom Petty's wildflowers,
the place where you belong.
How sweet the wind to anchor
you in the love of now, this

present tense, this lover of
be in this moment, marvel
in its luster and spark; sharp-
edged precipice, even footing.

Effloresce

Kersten Christianson

Today I broke the spine
of Mary Oliver's *A Poetry Handbook.*
while contemplating sound and device.

My finger traces its even seam, words laid
down like train track—aligned, avoiding dips,
spikes driven gently into the heartwood

of their meaning. The book's crack,
crumble, an alliterative soundtrack to the dog
outside eating dandelion greens

before their orgasm of bloom and seed.
And if this annual coming of bud and scatter
carries any real resonance, I imagine it

to moan like the night buoy at sea:
rounded, breathy, prolonged—late
into the dark morning hour.

It is book. It is paper. It is leaf.
Verdant, temporary, I ask,
Who hungers for you?

Meteors

Kersten Christianson

Named for star
patterns now obsolete
by time's ice fog, haze,
Quadrantids bloom
against the blackout

curtain of sky.
Picture their burst
of bud from dark soil
under imagined
constellations: box

kite, shark tooth,
flamingo's quill.
We nurture our
flourishing into
wild creativity.

Flora Universe

Will Neuenfeldt

Green stars
bright in

branches
suspend together

against the blue
void of sky.

At once,
all buds

supernova,
dusting space

with pollen
and shadow

where ladybugs
can study

the outer limits of
spring's galaxy.

Stone and Sky

Makaila Aarin

Boots shuffle over red dirt. Our linked arms
glisten beneath Arizona sun. Sparrows
whistle and glide. We pass families who swarm

Lookout Studio for telescopes
we used years ago, assuming the Canyon
behind a lens would appear more grandiose.

We approach a proudly protruding stone.
Pausing, throats dry, we sip from canteens.
I notice your top three blouse buttons undone.

You are feathers prickling my lungs lightly
when darkness crushes my chest without mercy.
You are the shrike shouting from clouds above
when I need more than a whisper of love.
You are blossoms of a prickly pear cactus
when grief drives deep and blisters feel ruthless.

While we stand on layered hues, your fingers
roll down my spine. My skin craves your caress.
I count cacti holding saffron treasures.

"Why do delicate blooms nest with needles?"
I ask, fitting my palm in your pocket, secure.
"Needles pierce tempted hands, preserve petals."

Your arm pulls my hip to yours. I sigh.
Your mulberry lips stamp my cheek. We smile
and savor six million years of stone and sky.

bird of paradise

Makaila Aarin

a bloom meant for oil on canvas,
exquisite but too wild to frame.

secretly toxic,

her petals mirrored a canary in flight,
fanned to fool me she'd stay faithful.

she fled as fast as she came.

dandelion

Makaila Aarin

Originally published in Stone of Madness Press

bold dandelion
bursts and blossoms through blacktop.
unwanted, but persistent.

Rebirth

Katie Oliver

She zips keys into the back pocket of her lumpy leggings and pulls her top down over her bum, wary of shouts from men in vans; the full-length mirror in the hallway adds an imposing backdrop to her preparations. None of this stuff had ever bothered her pre-baby, when she strode out in figure-hugging Lycra with a body that belonged solely to her.

She inches onto the street that swells with far too many people, heart rate up before any exercise has taken place. Last time she'd turned back before she'd reached the front door, slumping against the wall in preemptive humiliation. Today, at least, she has gone one step further. *This is progress*, she tells herself, a whispered affirmation that she clasps to her chest as she makes her way through the muddle of pedestrians and heads toward the quieter back streets.

She breaks into a faltering jog and feels every inch of the body that has told a thousand stories: the pain in her knees, the crunch in her hips, the slightly unstable pelvic floor. Each slap of shoe on concrete is a triumph, a validation. An escape. She runs past teenagers, families, dogs, all of whose existence is whipped away on the breeze as freedom begins to fizz through her veins. Bright pink blossoms scatter over her like confetti, and she laughs, violently grateful for the rasp of air in her lungs, the sound of her breath. The simple fact of a functioning body.

She runs through an underpass. The sunlight glancing off a puddle makes ripples on the wall and she stops, momentarily sucker-punched by the simple beauty of the effect. She turns and starts to run for home, hope poking out of her like a flower emerging from a broken patio.

Through the Eyes of a Three-Year-Old

Karen Ulm Rettig

Walking with my granddaughter in March,
still winter but feels like spring.
She tells me the trees are dead;
I pull down a branch to point out buds,
barely bumps, explain
that they are baby leaves.
On a bush we find more buds
like tiny brown pinecones.
I try to explain the process
in a child's language (forget photosynthesis)
start with tree sap (tree juice, tree blood)
how it lives in the roots all winter,
down in the warm ground, then travels
up the tree in spring, up the pipe
to make leaves. (I'm a little shaky
on the science, but it sounds about right.)
I tell her it will happen quickly;
brown bumps will become green leaves
or maybe flowers. She listens, credulous,
believing no matter how improbable
it sounds, because when you're three years old
magic is real, even when it's called science.

April, and I'm walking alone.
Those pinecone shapes have swelled
and leaves are shooting out the ends.
Some trees have exploded into bloom, snowing
petals onto the sidewalk, while others
have draped themselves in green lace.
In my mind, I'm pointing it all out
to my granddaughter, more aware
than I have been in years
that it's magic.

How to Get Home

Emily Rose Miller

After Philip Levine

Turn right off Kilkenny Way
       onto Epping Lane and recall
              what your babysitter once joked:

I remember your address because my brother's
       name is Kenny and sometimes I just wanna—
              See the line of manicured lawns and houses

in peach and yellow and green and stop
       in front of the one wearing brown.
              Not brown like dirty but brown

like dirt, like soil. Things grow here;
       you grew here, long ago, running
              around the yard avoiding oak roots

as your own personal dexterity training.
       Look at the newly placed concrete
              where the deep-pink crepe myrtle

shuddered and blossomed every year above
       her fragile bark and branching reach.
              Let it remind you of yourself; let the concrete

represent time—everything changes—and maybe
       the way it rips off innocence, too. How nature
              is so beautiful and sure of itself and time,

---

grasping hands with people, just snatches it
          away. But see, too, the new budding garden
                    along the left exterior wall, green shoots

the same as you at five years old—moving in,
          spinning cartwheels in the empty rooms—later
                    cozy in your seemingly forever bed, too excited

to sleep. If you stand there long enough, staring
          up the driveway, you can picture yourself a green bud,
                    swaying in the breeze, stretching
                    up to the ever-cycling sun.

picture yourself a green bud

In April, After I'm Twelve

Christine M. Estel

Straight up from the dark soil of green swishy pants and hot pink underwear around my ankles, my legs stemmed until the knees, where they bent and continued onward and inward, eventually converging at delicate petals bleeding for the first time. The stark contrast between red and wadded white tissue in my shaky hand stunned and scared me.

I never read the part about a girl's first cycle because I didn't have one of those books. My briefing came from the May before in fifth grade health class and an earlier conversation with my mother at the creepy, unmanicured park nestled in the dead end of a street in a neighboring town, a place I realized later was apropos for how I felt my mother handled my puberty—hiding, keeping it distanced, speaking only in whispers.

As we sat on the lone bench, I squirmed and sweated as she explained the changes that would happen to my body soon, if they hadn't already. Blushing, I avoided eye contact when I informed her, "Well, I already have those things." My body had already been budding pink-tipped porcelain bulbs and had been sprouting stamen a couple shades darker than I'd been expecting.

"Oh, okay. Your first one shouldn't be too much longer," she advised. And so I waited.

But even with the early signs of spring, I was unprepared for this moment. Panicked, I called her name in a worried whine, hoping the sound alone communicated what was happening so that I wouldn't have to speak.

"Whaaat?" she whined back, irritated.

"I got my period!"

Moments later, she creaked open the linen closet door, right outside the bathroom where I sat. Then she slid one pad through the crack in the door and waited outside until I emerged, frantic and furrowing my brow.

"At least it happened at home, right?" she said.

"I guess, but I have gym class today," I said as I dropped my head and looked to my feet.

After giving me the never-helpful *you'll be fine* with a tap on the shoulder, she continued downstairs to get my siblings ready for the car ride to school, leaving me with the mirror. In it, I saw myself—my blemished face covered in pink and white dots, unruly curly hair, unkempt eyebrows, and now the crimson stain of womanhood. Never impervious to ridicule, I wondered how something so ugly would get through the day unnoticed.

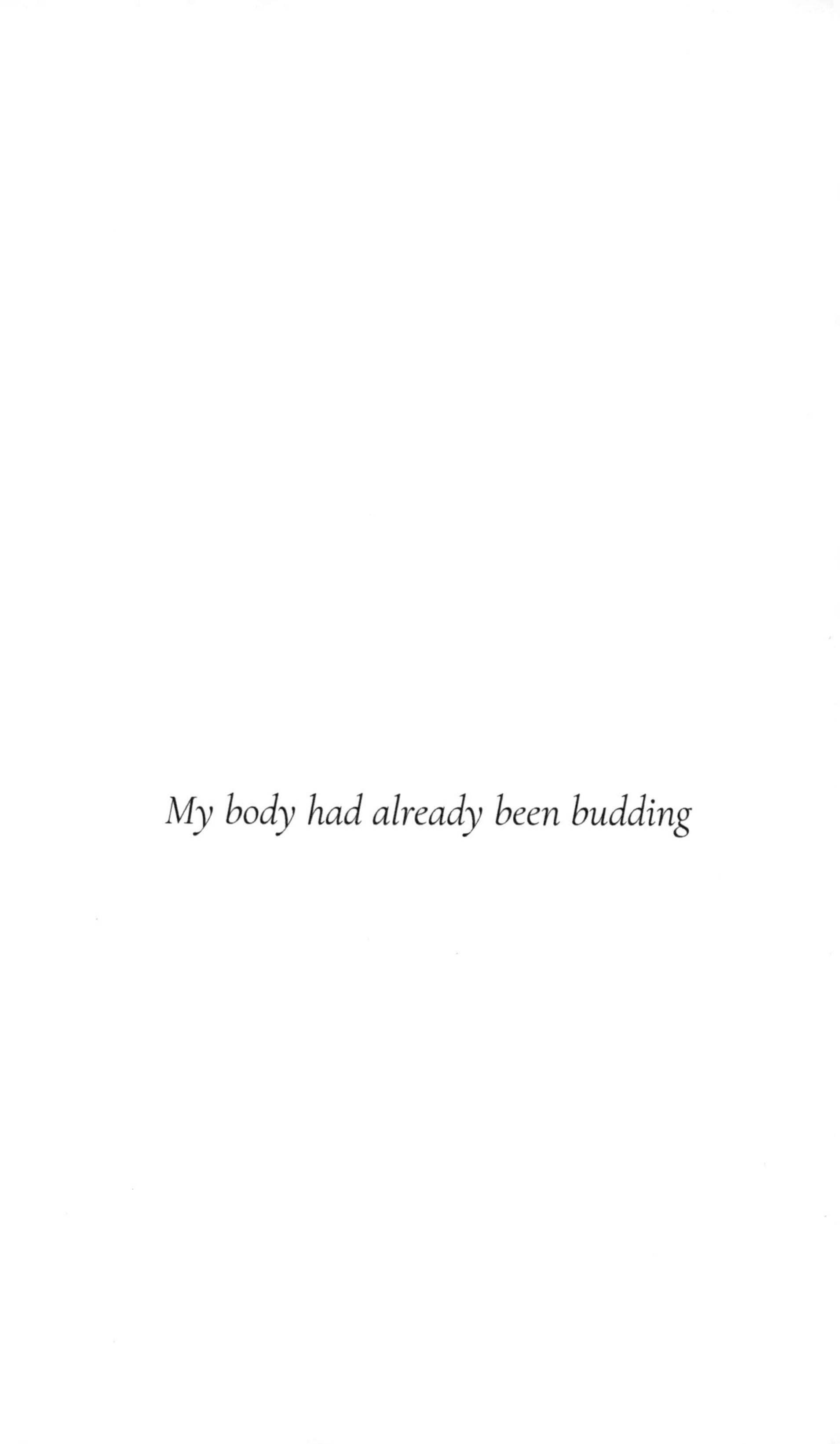

My body had already been budding

To Be in Bloom

Liz Russell

Everyone said
She was in bloom.
Flower blossom
Growing bosom
And changing every day.

Oh, Incipient Spring,
What they do not say!
Tightly wound bud
Every petal crushed
Until the shell gives way.

To Wilt

Raihana Haynes-Venerable

With my mind consumed
by body parts on screens,
I forgot to stop
to look at the flowers—life—
outside a cacophony of death.

I'm not sure if flowers feel their roots
in the same way I feel my own
body tingle when I am still.

Would flowers consent to being uprooted,
made fixtures on our mantels?

*If I am a flower,
my mother is the sun.*

Spring,
the purest embodiment of change,
frigidity to color, fragility to color.

We bloom into
familiarly unfamiliar realities
year after year after year after year.

I like to imagine a field of orange poppies
in place of the pavement that collected Brown's blood.

Cradling the final speck of Black innocence.

They say we are flowers because we are delicate.
Flowers are not delicate.

> I sometimes wonder why dandelions are
> considered weeds—a nuisance.
> Such brilliance
> in a design where a simple
> breath is rebirth.

Come back
          springtime.
          springhead.
          springtail.
          springtide.
          springlets.
          springwood.

> You were the rose, I the sunflower.
> Sisters, planted together,
> too close, trapped together.
> Stems interlaced
> your thorns, dug into my
> leaves. Stunted—both
> stunted.

I never tried
blocking the sun,
are you finally getting
enough?

> *If I am a flower,*
> *my father is the rain.*

I never wanted a bouquet of flowers
delivered to my front door, with a note
saying *I love you*—what is lovely in
the death of beauty?

What if those
six Black daisies
were allowed to
grow?

Abigail
Markis
Jeremiah
Sierra
Davonte
Hannah

Forgive us flowers for we have sinned.
Forgive us flowers for we have sinned.

I find it odd that
different colored roses have
different colored meanings.
Roses as stand-ins for love
roses, red, romance
roses, pink, grace
roses, yellow, joy
roses, white, innocence
roses, orange, excitement
roses, green, renewal
roses, black,

Oh, the lessons we'd
learn from pincushion cacti
in bloom, wide brimmed
in beams of light,
unexposed after nightfall.

As Black women we've been
conditioned to bloom
in winter months,
to provide life in desolation.

The petals pressed
inside the pages of
my teal moleskine,
souvenirs
of the lives I chose to take.

*flowers
are not delicate*

Brilliant Blue

Rebecca Ruvinsky

Red perfume on blue
lips, a spray of white
flowers tucked behind
the ear, the eyes closed
and painted with paleness.
Drink deeply of verdant
life, languishing green
sprouts dreaming of
the soil she will grow
into, when she is past
waiting and through
wearing her best.

I Pray and I Deceive

Hila Messer

I was just a seed when he met me
pulled me from the ground
and looked up close at the bruises on my skin
love is a dangerous thing, he said
while he examined the surface of my soul
wondering why I hadn't grown yet
you have to let go of the past, he said
and die in order to live again
isn't that violent? scary? irreversible?
I asked, looking up at his hungry eyes
he peeled my layers, one by one, and said
all great things are.

I was buried deep when she found me
consuming my own flesh
growing stronger than ever
but never blooming
she was scared like me and didn't have no advice
but she had wisdom in her eyes
and hope so bright
she reminded me of things I forgot I've known
one of her hands held mine
and the other covered faith's eyes
as we tricked the world into giving us
a gentle life
knowing we do not deserve it.

In which your toddler deserves a home without yelling.

L. Kardon

Your second spring was
brightly colored, and you
held on to it gently, sometimes
forgetful—the well-loved
stuffed animal always falling
in your wake as the daffodils
were dropping their petals.
The cherry-plum trees sent out
their little flowers.

The strawberries fruit early
in California and so by mid-
April your face was berry stained
at the table.

It was easy to be strong for
someone so innocent (and the
family had the means to help). By
lavender blossom time
we had left the little farm
to go it on our own. Finally,
an exhale, and the fragrance
of flowers for the next
breath in.

Elegy in Spring

L. Kardon

The wisteria, in its fleeting magic,
bloomed without you this year.
Still, it clings to the sycamore tree.
The blossoms wither and a sweet perfume,
everywhere, lingers.

We do not mourn the way you fit
in our home like shards of glass
in the garden bed—always bloodying
the tender's hands.

Nor do we miss
the little shivers of terror
up the spine of a soft bellied
beast when you'd bellow
your wrecking cry.

But in the tender moments, when the babe
is winsome and the lilacs rustle, fragrant,
in the wind,
there is a little emptiness
where your clamor used to go
that mourns its own
spacious, restful quiet.

Landscape Hymn

L. Kardon

There are new ponds
forming in old places
from the steady rains.
The branches are heavy
again with blossoms.

The new tender is soft
and precise, with hands
that reassure the soil.
Insects come to life. Awake,

the smooth hill-country,
ass, thighs, and breasts.
The rolling green
beneath birds, and
soft-stomping

fawns. Bushes bloom
among the sweetbriars.

Beetles glisten in the
rosebud. Awake,

the lightest touch,
teasing the grass.

A womanly gasp,
the land shudders

and swells. Everywhere,
sweet fruits drop,
past-ripe, open
to the fowl. Let flow

the wine, the nectar,
the milk-poppies
bursting. The flesh
of melons and
honey-heavy hives.

Berry-stained. The sweet
tasting morsels, awake.

the new tender is soft and precise

I Am Where I Am Going

Melissa Sussens

It is an art;
to unlearn that which once held my body upright,
to unknow each place her skin brushed against my own,
to live in the now and turn away from the then.
To wake up with the birds and make pancakes
for one on a Sunday. To not check my phone.
To not write *I still miss her*.

It is an exercise in resistance;
to train the mind to be less one tracked
or, to train the heart to be less muscle memory.
To not think about her on repeat, to stop
crying myself to sleep.
To realize for the first time
that happiness does exist
without her, as I make my morning tea
and pour out comfort.

It is knowing a place for the first time,
even if it belonged to us before;
the dam where we picnicked afternoons away,
the parking lot where we made out in my car,
the ice cream shop where she accidentally
dropped the words *I love you.*
That was a different life.

It is boxed away now.
I must resist the urge to pick it up
and wipe it off, to cradle it in my arms
like a child. Don't reread the love letters.

Don't scroll through our photos together.
These memories will not get me where I am going.

I am learning my face anew.
The curve, the angle, the mirror of me
an image I had forgotten.

Now, I trace the outline of the places
she did not make home.
I hold them close;
small, untouched treasures of relief;
the earlobe, the hip bone, all ten toes.
These belong to me and me alone.

She is not where I come from,
only a rest stop along the way.
I am where I am going.
My path is unknown,
but I know that I do not want
to just survive anymore.
I want life to touch me.
I want joy to find me.

I want to fall in love with a new woman
and lose her within a day of our meeting.
I want to walk aimlessly, past dark,
shaking with the emotion of the could-have-beens.
I want to not eat a bite on a first date
because my stomach is already full
of the *please let this be* . . .
I want to become all over again.

I want to become
all over again.

Become

Melissa Sussens

I.

If everyone I loved was dead
I could finally be truly lonely
without the guilt of knowing
that love for me exists.
I could wallow in my sadness,
cry myself a mountain stream
and not have to cross it.

II.

Maybe if I knew the girl
I once loved no longer
existed that fountain of hope
within me would finally dry up.

III.

I'd let my hair down,
get a tattoo. What would it say?

IV.

Become.

V.

Nothing is more permanent
than becoming. I remind myself
of this daily. If we're talking daily affirmations
I'd say breathing is the most important
one.

VI.

Resilient.
On the inside
of a wrist perhaps? Or over my heart,
a reminder of the unbreakable compass
I carry within.

VII.

Forgiveness.
The shape of the word
still a stretch to my lips,
perhaps could find a home
in my skin.

VIII.

I want to believe solely
in my own ability to overcome.
If you were all dead,
would I still be here?

IX.

I still become,
despite.
Even falling
I am fighting gravity,
to land within myself—
the perfect trampoline.

X.

I am made of springs,
carry the storm within.
With each day I am becoming
more resilient,
more able to forgive myself
for all that I am not,
for all that I am.

Early Spring

Sarah W. Bartlett

In this too-early spring,
greens thrusting upward full bore
as if to outwit the snow that may come,

hearts open to sun without
pondering the pleasure

of feet too-early planted
bare in dirt warming leaves
from their cocooned caves of cold,

concerns for the moment melted
in this burst of becoming.

Morning Rituals

Sarah W. Bartlett

Each morning, the same standoff
between dog and bunny frozen
watching the other in mutual curiosity,
or dare. My impatience to move along
breaks it up. Each morning
the same.

Each morning, the same peering
into thorned branches of red and amber
raspberries, thumb pressing confirmation
of ripeness; the blues likewise tested
and plucked, too-soon pink or pale green turning
deep purple-blue with time whether on or off
the branch. To the mouth, it's the same.

Each morning, the same need to release the dogs
to the yard, feed, then run them in the fields—
a pack of fur and feet that fetch what we toss,
return, repeat, swim like otters, roll in the grass;
each morning the white egret standing watch
in the next pond until we pass, tired,
and he returns to his peace. Each morning,
the same needs for action
and stillness.

Each morning, the same pull to the page, words
spilling and rearranging themselves in stanzas,
feelings nudging thoughts eager to find
their shape across the screen.
Each morning, the same.

Each morning, the same waking
to sun-washed sky, eager breeze—
caresses of rest and time conspiring
to create appetite for more.
Each morning, blessedly
the same.

caresses of rest and time conspiring

to create appetite for more

Hope Abundant

Sarah W. Bartlett

I.
It is our custom to leave the last bouquet
of late summer hydrangea on the table, fading
mauve globe beneath a wave of golden grass
speaking of passage. Come spring, a green sprig
leafed from withered stalk, nourished
by what water remained within.

II.
In this drawn-out time of drought,
the hydrangea, by day's end having endured
hot air and rising temperatures, wilts
defeated by the effort to stand tall;
by morning, clusters revived
to face what may come.

III.
The ancient clematis at the deck
was slashed at its husklike stalk
mistaken by the passing mower
for dead; but adversity only slows
and redirects new growth outward
from her withered vines.

IV.
The newly installed clematis
already clings to its trellis, turning
to view its new surrounds, a pile
of seed shells gathered and placed there
by the three-year-old hands of my grandson,
unwitting steward of the future.

V.
At Mimi's memorial I speak
of the necessity to plant gardens
wherever we live, her lesson embedded
beneath my nails, abundance
blossoming from her life to mine,
and far beyond.

abundance blossoming
from her life to mine

March

Ai Jiang

A wise tree sways in
front of every house. Although
static under ice

a month ago, now
dances, sprouting buds of leaves
and flowers whose shapes

and colors are still
unknown to the world around
them. The cautious ground

is slow to wake. Yet,
the end of their long slumber
grows near as the sun

no longer shines cold,
white light, but instead mellow
warmth and thawing breath

that breathes life on to
hard soil. At last, the soil wakes
along with the life

that waits beneath, but
withdraws into depths again
when March snow visits.

Bittersweet

Eileen Sateriale

a brisk autumn day
we gathered bittersweet
prized for its orange berries

the cold weather set in
yellow orange bittersweet
naked winter days

the torn blue quilt
snuggled your body
and kept you warm

I lowered the blinds
darkened the room
sat next to your bed

a bittersweet time
the light of spring came
a time of butterflies

you like spring
the season of rebirth
and gentler weather

yellow green flowers
grew quickly on
the bittersweet vine

you slept many hours
while the monitor
tracked your heartbeat

we held hands
warm wrinkled skin
time was short

I nodded off
when I opened my eyes
you had passed

it was early morning
I felt sad yet relieved
pain no more

it was a sad day
life celebration
bittersweet

*you like spring
the season of rebirth*

chrysanthemums

Ernest O. Ògúnyẹmí

---

do you know what it means to not belong in your own body?
I write this over and over in the sand that covers my mother's

bones. but the bones do not squeak, do not rewrite the soft
architecture of their laying. how easily I forget that the coin

my father tossed in the animal's body won't be found in the sea
of mine. on good days, the memory of my mother is a garden,

bright with untouched flowers. on others I find myself wandering
in a parched field—like Cain, like Adam before him. the list is long.

the history, a fat mouth—where an elegy of bats stunt without rest.
I wonder if she is here, my mother, under this piece of cold earth,

if she shares the space with her bones that lay, quiet as toothless
pianos. I was told the dead visit their dearest place on Wednesdays,

they trouble the curtains, disturb the kitchen, unquiet the sheets,
unpocket the drawers. when they're done stating their presence,

the dead, do they visit their graves? and there, atop the graves
that carry their names, soft gifts, do they drop chrysanthemums?

A Coffin Is Not a Cocoon

E. E. Rhodes

I thought of you this morning, so I write to you from our prayer-house of trees. I am sorry you are not here to enjoy them with me. The blossom of the apple has already been and gone, and the pink from the wild cherry is just clinging on. The may is in full flower, and the blackthorn is close behind. There are wrens nesting in the elder, which I do not think I have seen before. But the faithful robins have returned and I have heard the blackbird argue his corner, the same this year as the last.

There are gamboling swifts, high on the updrafts, as ever I fail to capture them on film or on the page, and I regret to say there are martins at the eaves. Regretted only because I know you loved them and that you would be glad to see them now. I think there are eggs, maybe hatchlings too.

The lilac, like me, is considering its ways, and though I know it made you sneeze, it is gearing up to be a full-bellied thing. The sycamore, too, has dangled its keys, unlocking the door to the next steep path of time. I am glad the mountain ash has survived thus far, and perhaps there will be jelly in the autumn. The medlar, I am sorry to say, is doing well. I know you had hoped to make more paste, though I still loathe that bletted smell.

Did I tell you before there is toadspawn in the pond? There is, and I can just manage to keep it topped up with water from the butt, for the weather has been dry and not minded to help. But I have seen the parents down at the compost heap, damp and slug-sleek green, and I am hopeful there will be more. No newts, to my knowledge, just these fine common toads.

The old vixen roams widely, but she returns each night and rests under the hedge. I still hope for kits, though the season may be late. I hope you would not scold me that I still leave her good chicken eggs. I've been listening, too, to the bats in the attic. One has made it down the chimney, which makes me wonder about brickwork holes. The house is fraying at the edges now, too often empty, too often cold.

Still, the crumbling mortar is all to the good for the masonry bees and there are solitaries around the house. The old skep is almost folded in on itself, but I hope something might still make it a home. There have been moths and butterflies already waking. And I saw one this week I did not know. I will try to send a picture to my friend, the insect man.

The turn of the year suggests I have been caterpillared for too long, one of the imminent moths, currently cocooned. You used to say that a coffin was not a cocoon. My dearest mama, what would you say now? Changed as you must be? Buried in the ground. The London clay is cracking, and all of us hope for rain, for the sound as well as the wet. I know the garden still misses you, as do I. But when I look around here at all this springing, living green, I tell myself the cocoon of the garden should not be a coffin, and that it may be time to fly.

I know the garden
still misses you,
as do I

If Flowers Could Speak

Lia Nizen

I want to know about underneathness,
the way the roots of a flower know the security of being unseen,
oblivious to the beautiful thing they've created on the other
side of the dirt.

I want to know about the flowers that fail to take root,
the ones that droop and drag along the ground,
plagued by a spinelessness they're unaware of.
I want to know what it's like to be consistent with work
regardless of success.
To break into bloom or fail and take root all the same.

Once, I planted celosia in my front garden,
a flocculent plume that took root in front of climbing ivy,
her bright magenta contrasting the pale blue creeping phlox.
After a month, her color faded and her branches wilted, leaving
her pot vacant.

Four months later, I discovered six seedlings pushing
their way through the rocks on the opposite side of the garden.
When my first celosia plant died, her heart was left behind,
waiting for the right time to start beating.
The wind had spread her love to the daisies and daylilies,
the petunias and peony, the lavender and larkspur.

Soon the celosia seedlings established themselves,
strong and vibrant like their mother plant.
I want to know if they understand what came before them,
if they know one of their own died so they could have life.

Still, Life (With Avocados)

Claire Taylor

She traced a knife around the outside of the avocado, pried the two halves apart with her fingers, and dug out the pit with a spoon. She would cube the soft green flesh before scooping it into the bowl, the way her mother taught her, so it would mash down easily, leaving zero lumps. Nice and smooth.

She would stick a toothpick into each side of the avocado pit and set the little contraption in a jar. The jar would sit on the windowsill in the dining room alongside all the others, avocado pits lined like votive candles at a prayer altar, though Elizabeth wasn't much for praying. She had hope, though. A little at least. She hadn't lost that completely in all of this. She hoped one of the pits would sprout soon, though none had yet and the entire enterprise was starting to feel like something you'd see on an episode of *Hoarders*—an unstable woman who spent her days gently cooing to her collection of avocado stones, pleading with them to show her some sign of life.

"You are not crazy," she'd whisper to herself in the gray hush of the early morning, whenever she woke before the sun, that strange feeling having suddenly returned to the hollow beneath her solar plexus. A flutter, a pulse, like the beating of a moth's wings against glass—the first signal of what lay ahead in the weeks to come, a steady downward spiral into darkness. The avocados helped, or she told herself they helped, and for now that was enough.

Half the battle was pretending you were okay. Waking up each morning to say, "Today will be fine." Trying to speak the words into existence, slowly letting the lie turn into truth.

It would be easier now that the weather was shifting, hard ground softening into damp earth. The promise of spring. Mornings that smelled of dirt, rebirth, possibility. It had been nine months. Long enough for a baby to have been conceived, gestated, pushed from her body and placed into the waiting cup of her arms, its fragile head and useless neck tucked against the warm curve of her engorged breast. But they hadn't been ready to have a baby and now they would never have one. Maybe *she* would, someday, with someone else, but never the two of them, blended together into one new soul.

That possible future, plus every other conceivable one and all those she could never even imagine, gone in an instant. Lost on impact along with him. Shattered glass and bent metal. Her whole life crushed beneath a single point of collision. She thought she too might die from the impact, the ripple effect into every corner of her life—the person she was, the one she would become, even the one she had been. That was perhaps the most surprising part, the way his absence changed her recollection of every conversation, every moment of strife. Why had she complained so much about always being the one to do laundry? *Come back*, she thought. *Take a different route, don't turn left and I promise I'll never mention the laundry again.* Had she told him she loved him often enough? Did she tell him every day? She should have told him every day. Every minute. Every time she thought, *I hate you*, she should have said aloud, *I love you*, instead. How unfair that you only learned what really mattered when it was too late. How unfair to mourn a version of him that would never exist more than she mourned the man she had known. To miss the possibility of his hands turning paper soft and wrinkled with age, more than the weight of his strong thigh slung across her hip at night.

She sunk the tines of a fork into the cubes of avocado and let the tension in her shoulders release a little more with each gentle smush.

The tree across the alley had begun to sprout. She could see it from her kitchen window, the tiny white buds like blemishes popping through the skin of the tree bark. It was one of those stinky trees—she could never remember what they were called—the little white flowers filling the air with a scent that made her nose scrunch up the moment she stepped outside to pull the garbage cans to the curb.

"Ah, the sweet smell of spring," he would joke each year, hands on his hips, sucking a deep breath in through his nose. This year it would have to be her, taking the deep breath, making the joke. It was so painful, all the ways the world kept reminding her of what she had lost.

It had been almost unbearable this winter. Trapped in the house all alone. All the empty spaces. It felt absurd that she ever believed their place was too small.

She had started talking to him after an unexpected winter storm left icicles draped across every tree branch and electric wire. "What do we do if the power goes out?" she had asked him, as if he was sitting beside her on the couch, right there, ready to answer. It wasn't a wish, not a call to some unseen realm where she believed he was listening, waiting for a distant day when she would join him. She thought that she could conjure him. If she asked the right questions, kept talking, an incessant babble that started in the morning and continued until she finally drifted to sleep at night, he would appear. She would bring him back, force him to stand in front of her and grab her by the shoulders the way he did that one night when they'd had too much to drink at Celeste's engagement party and she'd started a fight about why he hadn't proposed to her yet. On and on she went. She kept shouting at him through the closed bathroom door as he washed his face, brushed his teeth. Grabbed his arm as he went to pull back the covers and said, "No, let's talk about this. We don't go to bed angry." He'd cupped his hands around her shoulders and squeezed hard, too hard. "For fuck's sake, Liza. Just shut up and go to sleep."

The following week he'd asked her to marry him. He'd had the ring for three months.

Of course he never appeared, but after a week of drab weather and her nonstop chatter like the hum of a refrigerator filling the house with a steady, persistent sound, she thought she could see him. He was hazy at first, a form in the background of a close-up photograph, a blur of color and undefined shape. But then more and more he was there, moving through the house as he always had, standing beside her at the kitchen counter in the morning while she poured herself a bowl of cereal. She'd pour a second bowl and slide it over to him where it would stay all day, and into the next. Each day a new bowl was added until a week had passed and her countertop was clogged with bowls of soggy cereal and the house smelled of fetid milk.

"Oh, honey," Celeste had said when she swung by Elizabeth's house one evening with an already uncorked bottle of wine, a giant bag of peanut M&Ms, and a list of every action movie currently available on Netflix. She folded Elizabeth into the soft cushion of her body, quietly cleaned up the kitchen, gently suggested that perhaps a hobby would be helpful, something calming on which Elizabeth could focus her energy, like knitting or calligraphy.

Elizabeth had chosen the avocado pits instead. She imagined filling her yard with avocado trees, walking out in the morning—cool air, wet grass, soft golden light filtering through the leaves. With a basket on her arm, she'd slowly collect the ripening fruit. Maybe she would build a vegetable garden, plant a few berry bushes, turn her small yard into an orchard and live entirely off the land.

She stuck three toothpicks into the pit, filled a jar with water and gently set the avocado pit into place. She carried the jar into the dining room and shifted the other jars around on the windowsill to create space.

"Hello, my lovelies," she whispered to the jars. "Can you even believe this beautiful morning we're getting? What do you think about a bit of fresh air today?" She pushed open the window and a burst of cool, damp air rushed in. She inhaled it deeply. The sweet smell of spring. The scent of the world pushing forward, starting over. Of roots awakening, yawning and stretching their arms wide. Of green life blinking open in the sunlight.

She inspected each of the avocado pits for signs of growth. No roots snaking down into the water. No cracks in the smooth brown shells of the seeds. No tiny sprouts pushing skyward.

"You can do this," she said, gently touching the top of each pit with the tip of her finger. "Take your time. There's no rush." She would wait patiently. It was amazing, she thought, how sometimes the world changed in an instant, flipped upside down so that one second it looked one way and the next it was completely unrecognizable. And how other times it changed only by force, through steady deliberate effort, the quiet will to push forward again and again, up and out of the dark, to make a series of tiny cracks through the hard surface of the world, everything slowly bringing itself back to life. It was glorious really. Painful and heartbreaking, and quite nearly too much to bear, but beautiful in both its complexity and simplicity.

The avocado pits would grow. She could feel it. She believed it.

"You're doing fine," she said aloud. "Keep going. You're doing fine."

Contributors

Makaila Aarin works as an academic librarian in Mississippi where she lives with her three rescue dogs. She holds degrees in English, library science, and education. She is pursuing an MFA in creative writing. Her poetry has appeared in *Prismatica Magazine*, *Stone of Madness Press*, *Poetically Magazine*, *Dwelling Literary*, and other magazines. Her work is forthcoming in *Versification* and *Sinister Wisdom*. Find her on Twitter at @makaila_aarin.

Purnima Bala (she/they) is a writer and artist from India. Her poetry and fiction can be found in *Kahini Quarterly*, *Ellipsis Zine*, *MoonPark Review*, *mineral lit*, *Walled Women Magazine*, and others. Connect with her on Twitter and Instagram at @purnimabala.

Sarah W. Bartlett has authored two poetry chapbooks with Finishing Line Press, *Slow Blooming Gratitudes* (New Women's Voices Finalist #130, 2017) and *Into the Great Blue* (2011). Word-midwife, grandmother, and gardener, she celebrates nature's healing wisdom and the human spirit's landscapes. Additional work appears in *Adanna*, *Ars Medica*, *The Aurorean*, *Chrysalis*, *Colere*, *Lilipoh*, *Minerva Rising*, *Mom Egg Review*, *PMS poemmemoirstory*, *Women's Review of Books*, and numerous anthologies, including the award-winning *Women on Poetry* (McFarland & Co. Inc., 2012).

Emma Bider is a writer and PhD student living in Ottawa. She is currently fixated on identifying trees in her neighborhood. Emma's collection of short stories *We Animals* was published in December 2020. You can follow her on Twitter at @ebider.

AJ Buckle is a poet and teacher living in and writing from his apartment in Ottawa, Canada. He holds an honors BA in literature from the University of Ottawa. He enjoys listening to records and tending to his houseplants when not having an existential crisis. His work has previously appeared in *The Broken City* and *Joypuke*. You can find him at @ajbuckle1985 on Instagram.

K-Ming Chang / 張欣明 is a Kundiman fellow, a Lambda Literary Award finalist, and a National Book Foundation 5 Under 35 honoree. Her debut novel *Bestiary* (One World/Random House, 2020) was longlisted for the Center for Fiction First Novel Prize and named a New York Times Book Review Editors' Choice. More of her writing can be found at kmingchang.com.

Kersten Christianson is a raven-watching, moon-gazing, high school English-teaching Alaskan. She serves as poetry editor of the quarterly journal *Alaska Women Speak*. Her latest collection of poetry is *Curating the House of Nostalgia* (Sheila-Na-Gig Editions, 2020). Kersten holds an MFA from the University of Alaska. Visit kerstenchristianson.com.

Emily Iris Degn is an ecofeminist and published artist, poet, travel writer, sustainability writer, photographer, fiction writer, and essayist. Her creative work can be found in many places, including *Coffee People Zine, Lunch Ticket, About Place Journal, For Women Who Roar Issue 3, Beyond Words*, and *Coffin Bell*. She is from the San Juan Islands in the Pacific Northwest but currently lives in the middle of the Blue Ridge Mountains.

Christine M. Estel lives and writes in the Philadelphia area. She tweets from @EstellingAStory.

Q. (Quanishia) Gibson is a writer whose work centers womanhood, healing, and transcendence. She is the self-published author of *The Flowering Woman: Becoming and Being*, as well as other books of poetry. Gibson hosts a monthly writing community for women called TEND, and she is cofounder of the nonprofit intergenerational healing space The Daughters Den. She lives and writes in Ohio.

Madi Giovina writes poems and stories. She is a coeditor for *Backslash Lit*, submissions coordinator for *What Are Birds? Journal*, and the founder of Perennial Press. Madi lives in Philadelphia with her feisty cat, Shrimp. You can find her on Instagram at @cyberinsecurity.

Darcy Greenwood is a writer and editor for *Brilliant Star*, an award-winning children's magazine, and loves writing novels. She lives on a little farm in the Pacific Northwest with her husband, twin sister, and two poodle puppies.

Sue Hann lives in London. Her work was longlisted for the Spread the Word Life Writing Prize 2020. She won the Diana Woods Memorial Award in 2020. Her work has been published in journals such as *Popshot Quarterly*, *Longleaf Review*, *Multiplicity Magazine*, *Lunch Ticket*, *One Hand Clapping*, *Lunate*, *Ellipsis Zine*, *Fewer Than 500*, *Funny Pearls*, and *Litro Online*, as well as various flash fiction anthologies.

Raihana Jacqueline Haynes-Venerable is an artist, a photographer, a poet, and a scholar. She received her BA in critical theory and social justice at Occidental College in Los Angeles and her MFA in poetry at Mills College in Oakland, California. Her work focuses on the issue of what it means to exist in America as a queer Black femme, and she is specifically interested in interrogations of institutions and patriotism.

You can access her poetry and photo series "Places to Find the american Flag in Arizona" in *Granada Issue 1* and her poem "College Football" in *Penumbra Online*.

Ai Jiang is a Chinese-Canadian writer and poet who graduated with a BA in English literature from the University of Toronto and is a student at the Humber School for Writers. Her work has appeared in *Maudlin House* and is forthcoming in *Beyond Words*, *Star 82 Review*, and elsewhere.

L. Kardon is a poet and parent residing in Philadelphia. Look for them in upcoming issues of *Wizards in Space* and *Gyroscope Review*.

BEE LB is a writer creating delicate connections. They have been published in *Crooked Arrow Press*, *Red Queen Literary Magazine*, Badlung Press, *Capsule Stories Autumn 2019 Edition*, and *Local Honey Midwest*. They can be found, on occasion, posting excerpts of their poems on Instagram at @twinbrights.

Hila Messer is a high school student who's been writing ever since kindergarten (and never stopped). She is constantly inspired by her Jewish, Latin American, and Middle Eastern family, and her roots drive her to write from a place of awareness and reflection.

Emily Rose Miller is a graduate of Saint Leo University, where she received her BA in English with a specialization in creative writing. Her work has been published in *The Dollhouse Magazine*, *Parhelion Literary Magazine*, *Red Cedar Review*, and *Inklette*, among others. Find her online at emilyrosemiller.weebly.com, on Instagram at @actualprincessemily, or in real life cuddling with her five cats.

Will Neuenfeldt graduated in 2017 with an English degree from Gustavus Adolphus College, and his poems have been published in *Firethorne* and *Razor Literary Magazine*. He lives in Cottage Grove, Minnesota, making the most of quarantine in a quiet town by reading and sleeping.

Lia Nizen (she/they) is an ambitious spoken word poet out of Wilmington, North Carolina. Locally known by their stage name The Pierian Poet, they are often found hosting and performing at open mic events or teaching their writing workshop! Check out some of their work on Instagram at @thepierianpoet and their workshop @metanoia_workshops.

Ernest O. Ògúnyẹmí is a writer from Nigeria. His works have appeared or are forthcoming in *Tinderbox, Yemassee, The Indianapolis Review, Down River Road Review, The Lit Quarterly, The Dark Magazine, 20.35 Africa: An Anthology of Contemporary Poetry III, 34 Orchard, Erotic Africa: The Sex Anthology, Acumen, Glass, Lucent Dreaming, Memento: An Anthology of Contemporary Nigerian Poetry, Litro Magazine*, and elsewhere. He is the curator of *The Fire That Is Dreamed Of: The Young African Poets Anthology*. His tiny book of poems, *my mother died & I became _______*, is forthcoming from Ghost City Press. He is a reader at *The Masters Review* and *Palette Poetry* and an assistant editor at *COUNTERCLOCK Journal*.

Katie Oliver writes flash fiction, poetry, and short stories. She has been shortlisted for the Bridport Prize and the Bath Flash Fiction Award and was awarded an honorable mention in the Reflex Fiction Winter 2019 competition. She has further work published in various places, including *Popshot Quarterly, Molotov Cocktail, perhappened*, and *Ellipsis Zine*, and is a first reader for *The Forge Literary Magazine*. She can be found on Twitter at @katie_rose_o.

Karen Ulm Rettig earned a fine arts degree in college but discovered in her thirties that she was also a writer. She is a member of Cincinnati Writers Project and has published one book, *Finding God: Our Quest for a Deity and the Dragons We Meet on the Way*. You can find her online at karenulmrettig.com.

E. E. Rhodes is an archaeologist who accidentally lives in a castle in England, with her partner, many books, and a lot of mice in the wainscoting. She writes CNF, flash, and prose poetry to try to make sense of it all.

Rae Rozman (she/her) is a poet and educator in Texas. Her poetry often explores themes of queer love (romantic and platonic), loss, and education and has been published in several literary magazines and anthologies. An avid reader, Rae is often curled up in a sunny corner with a mug of coffee, a big white bunny, and a novel. You can find her on Instagram sharing poems, book reviews, and pictures of her two adorable rescue bunnies at @mistress_of_mnemosyne.

Liz Russell is a disaster recovery consultant by day and a writer and podcaster by night. She lives in upstate New York with her boyfriend, her pup, and three chickens that all look alike. Her work has been featured in *Kindred* and *Peach Velvet Mag*.

Rebecca Ruvinsky is a student, poet, and emerging writer in Orlando, Florida. She has kept a streak of writing a poem every day since 2016, with work published or forthcoming in *Wizards in Space, Prospectus, Sylvia Magazine, Underland Arcana,*

From the Farther Trees, and others. She loves baking cookies, watching rocket launches, and listening to music too loud. She can be found at @writeruvinsky.

Eileen Sateriale is a retired federal government analyst who writes in her spare time. She lives with her husband in Methuen, Massachusetts, and is the mother of two grown daughters who live in New York and London. She has had poetry, short stories, and travel articles published in print and online media.

Natalia A. Pagán Serrano is a poet from Puerto Rico. She resides in Oregon drenched in tree-magic and rain. She adores her fiancé, Daniel, and her cat, Esteban. Natalia's poems have been published in *PANK Magazine*, *Portland Review*, and *The Journal of Latina Critical Feminism*, among others.

Melissa Sussens (she/her) is a queer South African veterinarian and poet. Her work has appeared in *Germ Magazine*, *Ja. Magazine*, *Odd Magazine*, and *The Sock Drawer*, among others. She is a small animal vet by day and by night a poet and editor involved in Megan Falley's Poems That Don't Suck online writing courses. She lives in Cape Town with her girlfriend and their two dogs. Find her on Instagram at @melissasussens.

Claire Taylor (she/her) lives in Baltimore, Maryland, and online at clairemtaylor.com. Her work has been nominated for the Pushcart Prize and Best American Short Stories and has appeared in a variety of print and online publications. She is the creator of *Little Thoughts*, a monthly newsletter of original writing for kids.

Lotte van der Krol's favorite color is the green-blue of the sky on a clear day about an hour after the sun has set. Her short fiction has appeared in *Popshot Quarterly* and *The Cabinet of Heed*, and you can find more of her stories on lottevanderkrol.word press.com. She's also way too much on Twitter at @lottevdkrol.

Eli Vandell (they/them/theirs) is a poet and writer based in Washington, D.C. They are the recipient of the 2020 Joseph A. Lohman III Poetry Prize from George Mason University and the Academy of American Poets. Their work is featured in *The Forge, Pussy Magic, Entropy, Feral, The Temz Review, Poets. org*, and *Capsule Stories Autumn 2020 Edition*.

Katherine Wiles is a creative writing major at Cumberland University in Lebanon, Tennessee. Her poem "Speak Not to Me" was published in the American High School Poets' *My World* anthology in October 2019. Her favorite parts of spring are being warm again and seeing everything turn green.

Editorial
Staff

Natasha Lioe, Founder and Publisher

Natasha Lioe graduated with a BA in narrative studies from University of Southern California. She's always had an affinity for words and stories and emotions. Her work has appeared in *Adsum Literary Magazine* and *Capsule Stories*, and she won the Edward B. Moses Creative Writing Competition in 2016. Her greatest strength is finding and focusing the pathos in an otherwise cold world, and she hopes to help humans tell their unique, compelling stories.

Carolina VonKampen, Publisher and Editor in Chief

Carolina VonKampen graduated with a BA in English and history from Concordia University, Nebraska and completed the University of Chicago's editing certificate program. She is available for hire as a freelance copyeditor and book designer. For more information on her freelance work, visit carolina vonkampen.com. Her writing has appeared in *So to Speak*'s blog, *FIVE:2:ONE*'s #thesideshow, *Moonchild Magazine*, and *Déraciné Magazine*. Her short story "Logan Paul Is Dead" was nominated by *Dream Pop Journal* for the 2018 Best of the Net. She tweets about editing at @carolinamarie_v and talks about books she's reading on Instagram at @carolinamariereads.

April Bayer, Reader

April Bayer is an MA student in English literature at the University of South Dakota. She graduated with high distinction from Concordia University, Nebraska in 2019 with a BA in English and theology and a BS Ed in educational studies. When she isn't busy teaching her students about literature and composition, she enjoys writing poetry, playing with cats, and researching the works of Willa Cather. Her work has previously appeared in *Potpourri* and *Capsule Stories*. April joined *Capsule Stories* as a reader in November 2020.

Hannah Fortna, Reader

Hannah Fortna graduated in 2016 from Concordia University, Nebraska, combining her passion for the written word and her affinity for art making with a degree in English and a minor in photography. After a three-year career as a freelance copyeditor, she heard traveling calling her name and now works seasonal jobs in places connected to America's national parks. When she's not selling souvenirs to tourists in gift shops, she enjoys hiking, photographing natural spaces, and writing about the flora and fauna she saw while on the trail. She reads anything from poetry to middle-grade novels, but the nature-inspired creative nonfiction section is her haunt in any bookstore. Her poetry has previously appeared in *Moonchild Magazine* and *Capsule Stories*. Hannah joined *Capsule Stories* as a reader in November 2020.

Submission Guidelines

Capsule Stories **is a print literary magazine** published once every season. Our first issue was published on March 1, 2019, and we accept submissions year-round.

Become published in a literary magazine run by like-minded people. We have a penchant for pretty words, an affinity to the melancholy, and an undeniably time-ful aura. We believe that stories exist in a specific moment, and that that moment is what makes those stories unique.

What we're really looking for are stories that can touch the heart. Stories that come from the heart. Stories about love, identity, the self, the world, the human condition. Stories that show what living in this world as the human you are is like.

We accept short stories, poems, and remarkably written essays. For short stories and essays, we're interested in pieces under 3000 words. You may include up to five poems in a single poetry submission, and please send only one story or essay at a time. Please send previously unpublished work only, and only submit to one category at a time. Simultaneous submissions are okay, but please let us know if your submission is accepted elsewhere. Please include a brief third-person bio with your submission, and attach your submission in a Word document (no PDFs, please!).

Find our full submission guidelines and current theme descriptions at capsulestories.com/submissions. You can email your submission to us at submissions@capsulestories.com.

Connect with us!
capsulestories.com
@CapsuleStories on Twitter and Facebook
@CapsuleStoriesMag on Instagram